PRINCEWILL LAGANG

Love in the Digital Age

First published by PRINCEWILL LAGANG 2023

Copyright © 2023 by Princewill Lagang

All rights reserved. No part of this publication may be reproduced, stored or transmitted in any form or by any means, electronic, mechanical, photocopying, recording, scanning, or otherwise without written permission from the publisher. It is illegal to copy this book, post it to a website, or distribute it by any other means without permission.

Princewill Lagang asserts the moral right to be identified as the author of this work.

First edition

This book was professionally typeset on Reedsy. Find out more at reedsy.com

Contents

1. Love in the Digital Age — 1
2. Love in the Digital Age — 5
3. Love in the Digital Age — 10
4. Love in the Digital Age — 14
5. Love in the Digital Age — 18
6. Love in the Digital Age — 22
7. Love in the Digital Age — 27
8. Love in the Digital Age — 31
9. Love in the Digital Age — 35
10. Love in the Digital Age — 40
11. Love in the Digital Age — 44
12. Love in the Digital Age — 48

1

Love in the Digital Age

The Transformative Impact of Technology on Modern Love

Introduction

In the grand narrative of human existence, love has always been a central theme—a force that binds us, drives us, and gives meaning to our lives. Across centuries and civilizations, love has been celebrated in poems, songs, and stories as an enduring, enigmatic, and ever-evolving aspect of the human experience. And today, in the midst of a digital revolution that has reshaped every facet of our lives, love finds itself in a remarkable new landscape—a landscape where the boundaries between the physical and digital worlds blur, and where our screens play an increasingly pivotal role in shaping romantic connections.

This is the age of love in the digital era, where the concept of modern romance has been profoundly transformed by technology. It's an era where we can swipe right or left to find potential partners, send emojis and GIFs to express our affections, and hold intimate conversations through the glowing screens of our devices. It's an era where love letters have been replaced by text messages, where virtual dates have become commonplace, and where online relationships are no longer a curiosity but a fundamental part of our social fabric.

But what does it truly mean to love and be loved in this digital age? How has technology impacted the way we form connections, express affection, and sustain relationships? What challenges and opportunities lie in this brave new world of love that exists in the digital ether? These are the questions that "Love in the Digital Age" seeks to answer as we embark on a captivating journey through the intricacies of modern romance in the era of screens and algorithms.

The Transformation of Love

Love has always been a reflection of the times in which it exists. It has evolved from arranged marriages and courtly love in centuries past to the free-spirited love of the counterculture in the 1960s. In each era, societal norms, cultural shifts, and technological advancements have shaped the contours of love, influencing how we meet, connect with, and understand one another.

Today, the digital revolution stands as one of the most influential factors in the evolution of love. We live in a world where technology has not only facilitated the way we communicate but has also expanded our reach, broadened our horizons, and brought us closer to potential partners than ever before. The digital age has given rise to online dating platforms that have revolutionized how we initiate romantic connections, explore our options, and seek companionship.

The Age of Online Dating

Online dating, once regarded with skepticism, has now become a mainstream avenue for meeting potential partners. The simplicity of swiping right to express interest or swiping left to pass on someone has transformed the dating landscape. We have seen the rise of algorithms that analyze our preferences and behaviors, attempting to match us with individuals who align with our desires and interests. The virtual realm has opened doors to endless possibilities, introducing us to people we might never have met otherwise.

In this digital age, online dating platforms have become the modern-day equivalent of bustling town squares, where individuals of diverse backgrounds, interests, and desires converge. Whether you seek companionship, romance, or something more, the digital world offers a diverse array of potential connections, each with their unique stories and aspirations.

The Promise and Perils of Virtual Intimacy

Yet, as we embark on this exploration of love in the digital age, we must also confront the complexities and contradictions that come with it. While technology has enabled us to connect with people across continents and oceans, it has also introduced unique challenges. Virtual intimacy, for all its promise, can sometimes feel like a double-edged sword—a bridge that connects, yet sometimes a barrier that separates.

Our screens, while allowing us to communicate and connect, can also become barriers to authentic connection. The art of building meaningful relationships in virtual spaces requires new skills and an understanding of the nuances of digital communication. It necessitates a willingness to navigate the challenges and benefits of virtual love, to strike a balance between the digital and physical realms, and to foster genuine connections in a world where screens mediate our interactions.

This journey through "Love in the Digital Age" will guide us through these intricate landscapes of modern romance. We will explore the art of crafting authentic profiles in the digital dating world, navigate the challenges and benefits of virtual relationships, and delve into the complexities of effective online communication. We will address trust and transparency in the digital realm, offer strategies for resolving conflicts that arise in digital interactions, and explore the delicate balance between our real and virtual lives.

As we embark on this journey, let us remember that love, in all its forms, remains the beating heart of our human experience. It endures, adapts, and thrives in the face of technological revolutions, cultural shifts, and societal changes. The screen may be a new canvas for love, but the emotions it conveys and the connections it fosters are as genuine, profound, and enduring as those that have bound humans together throughout history.

In the chapters that follow, we will embark on an exploration of love that transcends screens and algorithms, reminding us that amidst the complexities of the digital age, love remains a timeless force—a force that has the power to connect hearts, bridge distances, and illuminate our lives in ways both old and new.

2

Love in the Digital Age

Exploring the Landscape of Online Dating Platforms

Introduction

In our exploration of love in the digital age, we find ourselves standing at the crossroads of a profound transformation: the world of online dating. The digital revolution has not only redefined the way we communicate but also the way we seek companionship and romantic connection. It has given rise to a landscape of online dating platforms that serve as virtual gateways to the complex world of modern romance.

This chapter serves as our gateway into this digital realm, where algorithms, profiles, and swipes have become the tools of the trade. We will explore the fascinating landscape of online dating, gaining insight into its evolution, its impact on how we form relationships, and the strategies that empower us to navigate this world with authenticity and success.

The Evolution of Online Dating

Online dating, once a novel concept, has become an integral part of the modern love story. It has transcended its initial stigma to become a ubiquitous and accepted means of seeking love and companionship. But how did we arrive at this point? To understand the present, we must first trace the evolution of online dating from its humble beginnings.

1.1. A Brief History

Online dating's roots can be traced back to the early days of the internet. In the 1960s, Stanford students used primitive computer systems to match individuals for social events. Fast forward to the 1990s, and the world witnessed the emergence of the first online dating websites. These early platforms paved the way for a digital dating revolution.

1.2. The Rise of Dating Apps

The real game-changer came with the advent of dating apps in the late 2000s. Platforms like Tinder, Bumble, and OkCupid transformed the dating landscape. The simplicity of swiping right or left to indicate interest or disinterest revolutionized how we initiate romantic connections. These apps brought the world of online dating to the palms of our hands, making it accessible, convenient, and mainstream.

1.3. The Algorithmic Matchmaker

At the heart of modern online dating is the algorithmic matchmaker. These complex mathematical formulas analyze our preferences, behaviors, and profiles to suggest potential matches. As we engage with these platforms, we unknowingly provide data that informs the algorithms, guiding us toward individuals who align with our desires and interests.

Crafting Authentic Profiles

Online dating is, in many ways, a curated experience. Our digital profiles serve as our first impression, and they play a crucial role in attracting potential partners. Crafting an authentic, compelling, and genuine profile is a fundamental skill in the digital dating world.

2.1. Profile Photos

The visual aspect of online dating is undeniable. Profile photos are the first thing potential matches see, and they hold significant weight in the decision to swipe right or left. Selecting the right photos that represent your true self is a crucial step in attracting like-minded individuals.

2.2. The Art of the Bio

Beyond photos, your dating profile bio provides an opportunity to showcase your personality, interests, and what you're seeking in a potential partner. It's a chance to convey your authenticity and create a connection beyond the surface.

2.3. Honesty and Authenticity

In a world where it's easy to embellish or misrepresent oneself, honesty is your strongest ally. Authenticity in your profile not only attracts individuals who resonate with your true self but also sets the foundation for genuine connections.

Navigating Digital Dating Etiquette

As we immerse ourselves in the world of digital dating, it's essential to understand and abide by the unwritten rules and etiquette that govern this space. These guidelines can make the difference between a positive and successful online dating experience and one fraught with missteps and misunderstandings.

3.1. Initiating Contact

The first step in online dating is initiating contact with a potential match. Whether it's sending a thoughtful message or responding to a mutual match, the way you begin your digital interactions sets the tone for the relationship.

3.2. Respect and Communication

Respectful and open communication is at the heart of successful digital dating. Treat others with kindness and consideration, just as you would in face-to-face interactions. Effective communication is key to building a connection that can withstand the digital distance.

3.3. Handling Rejection

Rejection is an inherent part of online dating. Not every connection will lead to a meaningful relationship, and that's perfectly normal. Learning to handle rejection with grace and resilience is a valuable skill that will serve you well in the digital dating world.

3.4. Safety and Privacy

Online safety is paramount in digital dating. Protecting your personal information and being cautious about sharing sensitive details are crucial practices. We will delve deeper into the realm of online safety in later chapters.

Conclusion

As we conclude our journey through the landscape of online dating in "Love in the Digital Age," we are equipped with a deeper understanding of how technology has reshaped the way we meet potential partners. We have explored the evolution of online dating from its early beginnings to the era of dating apps and algorithmic matchmakers. We have learned the art of crafting authentic profiles and navigating digital dating etiquette with grace and respect.

But this is only the beginning. The digital dating world is vast, with its own unique joys, challenges, and nuances. In the chapters that follow, we will dive deeper into the world of virtual courtship and connection, uncovering the art of building meaningful relationships in virtual spaces, and addressing the unique challenges and benefits of digital romance. So, as we step further into the digital realm of love, let's embrace this exciting journey and discover the boundless possibilities it holds for each of us.

3

Love in the Digital Age

Virtual Courtship and Connection

Introduction

As we navigate the complex landscape of love in the digital age, we find ourselves standing at the threshold of a fascinating dimension of modern romance: virtual courtship and connection. In this chapter, we will explore the art of building meaningful relationships in the digital realm, where screens mediate our interactions, and geography often fades into the background. We will delve into the challenges and benefits of virtual love, discovering the unique dynamics that shape this evolving aspect of modern relationships.

Virtual Love: Navigating the Challenges

In the digital era, virtual connections have become an integral part of our love stories. The possibilities are endless: you might meet someone on a dating app from a different city or country, develop feelings through text messages, or form a deep emotional bond with someone you've never met in person. But with these opportunities come unique challenges that require careful consideration.

1.1. Geography and Time Zones

One of the defining features of virtual love is that it often spans geographical distances and time zones. While technology connects us, the reality of physical separation can create logistical and emotional challenges. Navigating the complexities of coordinating schedules, dealing with long-distance yearning, and bridging the gap between different time zones can be demanding.

1.2. Building Trust from Afar

Trust is the cornerstone of any successful relationship, and this holds true in the digital realm. Building trust when you can't physically be present is a unique challenge. Overcoming doubts, addressing insecurities, and fostering open communication are essential for creating a foundation of trust in virtual love.

1.3. Balancing Virtual and Physical Connection

In virtual relationships, it's crucial to strike a balance between the digital and physical realms. While virtual connections can be fulfilling, they can't replace the richness of in-person experiences. Finding ways to maintain intimacy and closeness while apart is a continuous endeavor.

1.4. The Role of Technology

Technology, while a powerful enabler, can sometimes create misunderstandings or miscommunication. The nuances of facial expressions, body language, and tone can be lost in text-based conversations. Learning to navigate these challenges and adapt your communication style to the digital context is vital.

The Benefits of Virtual Love

While virtual love comes with its own set of challenges, it also offers unique benefits and opportunities that enrich our modern romantic experiences.

2.1. Emotional Intimacy

Virtual connections often place a strong emphasis on emotional intimacy. When physical presence is limited, individuals tend to share their thoughts, feelings, and vulnerabilities more openly. This depth of emotional connection can lead to profound bonds.

2.2. Deep Communication

The digital realm encourages deep and meaningful communication. Without the distractions of physical surroundings, conversations can be focused, honest, and introspective. This quality of communication can strengthen connections.

2.3. Exploration and Discovery

Virtual love allows us to explore and discover individuals from diverse backgrounds and cultures. It opens doors to a world of possibilities, helping us broaden our horizons and challenge our preconceived notions about love and relationships.

2.4. Flexibility and Adaptability

Virtual love requires adaptability and flexibility. Navigating the challenges of long-distance connections or differing time zones can teach us valuable life skills and the ability to adapt to changing circumstances.

Conclusion

As we conclude our exploration of virtual courtship and connection in "Love in the Digital Age," we find ourselves on the brink of a new understanding of modern romance. We have delved into the challenges and benefits of virtual love, recognizing that while screens may mediate our interactions, the emotions and connections formed in the digital realm are as real and meaningful as those forged in physical spaces.

In the chapters that follow, we will continue our journey through the intricacies of love in the digital age. We will explore the art of effective online communication, uncover the role of trust and transparency in the digital realm, and offer strategies for resolving conflicts that arise in digital interactions. Together, we will navigate this evolving landscape of love, forging connections that transcend the boundaries of screens and algorithms, and discovering the profound depths of human emotion in the digital era.

4

Love in the Digital Age

Navigating Online Communication

Introduction

In the intricate tapestry of modern romance, effective communication stands as the warp and weft, weaving together the threads of connection and understanding. As we continue our exploration of love in the digital age, we find ourselves at a crucial junction: the realm of online communication. In this chapter, we will delve into the complexities of communicating effectively in the digital context, where texts, emojis, GIFs, and screens shape our interactions. We will unravel the nuances of this digital language, exploring how tone, context, and emotional intelligence play pivotal roles in fostering meaningful connections.

Effective Communication in the Digital Era

Effective communication has always been at the heart of any successful relationship. In the digital age, where the majority of our interactions happen through screens and keyboards, the art of conveying thoughts, emotions, and intentions takes on a unique form. Let's explore the principles and practices of effective online communication.

1.1. The Power of Words

Words are the building blocks of communication, and in the digital realm, they are your primary tools for expressing yourself. The brevity of text messages and online chats places added emphasis on choosing your words thoughtfully. Effective online communication entails clarity, conciseness, and consideration.

1.2. Emojis and Visual Language

Emojis, GIFs, and stickers have become integral to digital conversations. These visual cues add depth and emotion to your messages, bridging the gap left by the absence of facial expressions and body language. Understanding the nuances of this visual language is essential for conveying tone and intent.

1.3. Context Matters

Context plays a crucial role in online communication. A single sentence can have vastly different meanings depending on the context in which it is presented. Recognizing when to be serious, when to inject humor, and when to offer support is a skill that deepens your connections.

1.4. Emotional Intelligence

Emotional intelligence, the ability to recognize and manage your emotions and those of others, is a cornerstone of effective online communication. It enables you to respond empathetically, navigate conflicts with grace, and build trust in digital relationships.

The Role of Tone and Context

One of the most significant challenges in digital communication is the absence of tone and non-verbal cues. In face-to-face conversations, tone of voice, facial expressions, and body language provide critical context and emotional depth to our words. In the digital realm, it's essential to understand how tone and context influence the meaning of your messages.

2.1. Conveying Tone

Conveying tone accurately in digital messages can be challenging. A message intended as light-hearted humor may come across as sarcasm without the appropriate context. Using emojis, punctuation, and explicit language can help clarify your intended tone.

2.2. Misunderstandings and Assumptions

Misunderstandings are common in digital communication. It's easy for recipients to misinterpret messages when they lack the context or visual cues to understand your intent. Avoiding assumptions and seeking clarification when necessary can prevent unnecessary conflicts.

2.3. Active Listening in Digital Conversations

Active listening is a valuable skill in digital interactions. It involves not only reading the words but also paying attention to the emotions and nuances behind them. Asking questions and seeking to understand the other person's perspective are essential components of active listening in the digital era.

2.4. The Art of Digital Empathy

Empathy is the ability to understand and share the feelings of another. In digital communication, empathy is a powerful tool for building connections and resolving conflicts. Expressing understanding and support, even through screens, can foster emotional closeness.

Conclusion

As we conclude our exploration of online communication in "Love in the Digital Age," we have unraveled the intricacies of effective digital interaction. We have recognized the power of words, the significance of visual language, and the role of context in shaping our online conversations. We've explored the challenges of conveying tone and the importance of emotional intelligence in building meaningful connections.

In the chapters that follow, we will continue our journey through the ever-evolving landscape of love in the digital age. We will examine the impact of social media on dating and relationships, explore strategies for maintaining healthy boundaries and authenticity online, and delve into the redefinition of intimacy through technology and virtual experiences. As we navigate this digital realm of love, let us remember that effective communication, whether through words or symbols, remains the bridge that connects hearts across screens and algorithms, forging connections that transcend the boundaries of the virtual world.

5

Love in the Digital Age

Social Media's Role in Modern Romance

Introduction

As we delve deeper into the realm of love in the digital age, we come face to face with a powerful force that has profoundly shaped modern relationships: social media. In this chapter, we will examine the impact of social media on dating and love, exploring the ways in which platforms like Facebook, Instagram, Twitter, and TikTok have revolutionized the landscape of romance. We will also discuss strategies for maintaining healthy boundaries and authenticity online while navigating the complexities of a world where likes, shares, and followers play a role in shaping our love stories.

The Impact of Social Media on Dating and Relationships

Social media has permeated nearly every aspect of our lives, and love and relationships are no exception. Let's explore the multifaceted ways in which social media has left its mark on modern romance.

1.1. Connecting Across Distances

One of the most significant benefits of social media is its ability to connect people across vast distances. Long-distance relationships can be sustained through real-time chats, video calls, and the sharing of daily moments via platforms like Instagram Stories or Snapchat.

1.2. Digital Courtship

Social media has become a space for digital courtship, where individuals express their interest in potential partners through likes, comments, and direct messages. It has transformed the way we initiate romantic connections, making it easier to express interest and get to know someone before meeting in person.

1.3. Relationship Status and Public Validation

The "relationship status" feature on platforms like Facebook and the act of sharing couple photos on Instagram have become symbols of public validation and commitment. These digital gestures are often seen as significant milestones in modern relationships.

1.4. Maintaining Connections

Social media helps us maintain connections with our partners and loved ones. It provides a platform for sharing updates, sending private messages, and staying connected even in the busiest of times.

Strategies for Maintaining Healthy Boundaries and Authenticity Online

While social media offers numerous benefits for modern romance, it also presents challenges related to privacy, authenticity, and boundaries. Here are some strategies to navigate the complexities of love in the age of social media.

2.1. Define Your Boundaries

Establish clear boundaries with your partner regarding what is acceptable to share online and what should remain private. Discuss your comfort levels with public displays of affection and decide how you want to present your relationship to the digital world.

2.2. Be Mindful of Over-Sharing

While it's natural to want to share the highlights of your relationship, be mindful of oversharing personal or intimate details. Consider the potential impact of your posts on both your partner and your online audience.

2.3. Digital Etiquette

Practice good digital etiquette by respecting your partner's boundaries and seeking their consent before sharing anything related to your relationship. Be considerate of their comfort levels in the digital realm.

2.4. Authenticity Matters

In a world where curated images and posts dominate social media, authenticity stands out. Be genuine in your interactions and posts. Share both the ups and downs of your relationship, as it's these authentic moments that often resonate most with your online community.

2.5. Communication is Key

Effective communication is the cornerstone of maintaining healthy boundaries and authenticity online. Regularly discuss your digital habits and feelings with your partner to ensure you are both on the same page.

Conclusion

As we conclude our exploration of social media's role in modern romance in "Love in the Digital Age," we have recognized its transformative impact on how we connect, court, and maintain relationships. We've explored the ways in which social media can bridge geographical distances, serve as a platform for digital courtship, and play a role in public validation.

Yet, we've also emphasized the importance of maintaining healthy boundaries and authenticity online. In the digital age, where it's easy to get caught up in the pursuit of likes and validation, it's vital to remember that true connections are built on authenticity, trust, and communication.

In the chapters that follow, we will continue our journey through the complex landscapes of love in the digital era. We will explore the redefinition of intimacy through technology and virtual experiences, delve into the challenges of trust and transparency in digital relationships, and discuss strategies for addressing conflicts that arise in digital interactions. As we navigate this digital realm of love, let us carry forward the wisdom that authenticity and communication remain the foundations of lasting and meaningful connections, whether they exist in the physical world or flourish in the virtual embrace of social media.

6

Love in the Digital Age

Love and Intimacy in the Digital World

Introduction

As our journey through "Love in the Digital Age" continues, we find ourselves exploring a profound dimension of modern romance: the redefinition of intimacy through technology and virtual experiences. In this chapter, we will delve into the intricate ways in which technology has transformed the landscape of emotional and physical closeness. We will examine how we cultivate intimacy in an era of digital connections, exploring both the benefits and challenges that come with this evolution.

Redefining Intimacy through Technology

Intimacy has long been a cornerstone of romantic relationships. It encompasses emotional closeness, vulnerability, and the unique bond that forms between two people who share their innermost thoughts and desires. In the digital age, technology has redefined how we experience and express intimacy.

1.1. Emotional Closeness

Technology has expanded our capacity for emotional closeness. Through digital channels, we can share our deepest fears, dreams, and joys with partners and loved ones, even when physical distances separate us. Virtual spaces become forums for emotional support and connection.

1.2. Visual and Sensory Experiences

The advent of video calls and virtual reality (VR) has brought visual and sensory experiences into the realm of digital intimacy. Couples can now share moments in real time, from virtual dates to exploring new places through VR headsets.

1.3. The Digital Love Language

Digital interactions have given rise to a new love language, where sharing memes, sending heartfelt texts, or creating playlists for your partner become meaningful acts of affection. These digital expressions of love can be as profound as physical gestures.

1.4. Overcoming Physical Separation

For individuals in long-distance relationships, technology serves as a lifeline. Video chats, messaging apps, and even synchronized movie-watching platforms enable couples to bridge the gap and maintain a sense of togetherness.

The Challenges and Benefits of Virtual Intimacy

While technology enhances our capacity for intimacy, it also presents unique challenges. Let's explore both the benefits and potential pitfalls of virtual intimacy.

2.1. Benefits

- Accessibility: Virtual intimacy transcends physical limitations, allowing individuals of diverse backgrounds and abilities to experience closeness.
  - Flexibility: Digital intimacy can adapt to various schedules and time zones, making it easier for couples to connect despite busy lives.
  - Creativity: Technology fosters creative expressions of intimacy, from sending surprise virtual gifts to sharing playlists that reflect your emotions.

2.2. Challenges

- Screen-Mediated: Virtual intimacy is screen-mediated, which can create a sense of disconnection or detachment compared to physical presence.
  - Digital Distractions: The same devices used for virtual intimacy can become sources of distraction, potentially taking away from the quality of connection.
  - Privacy Concerns: Sharing personal and intimate moments online raises concerns about privacy and the potential for data breaches.

Cultivating Emotional Closeness in the Digital Age

Building and maintaining emotional closeness in the digital age requires intention, effort, and a deep understanding of the digital landscape. Here are some strategies for cultivating intimacy in the world of digital connections.

3.1. Regular Communication

Consistent and open communication remains essential in cultivating emotional closeness. Make time for virtual check-ins, share your thoughts and feelings, and actively listen to your partner or loved ones.

3.2. Virtual Dates and Experiences

Plan virtual dates or experiences that simulate physical togetherness. Whether it's watching a movie together online, cooking the same meal over video chat, or exploring virtual worlds, these activities can help create shared memories.

3.3. Managing Digital Boundaries

Establishing digital boundaries is crucial. Discuss what you're comfortable sharing online and what should remain private. Respect your partner's boundaries and seek their consent when sharing personal moments.

3.4. Disconnecting When Necessary

Recognize the importance of disconnecting from technology when it's time to focus on your partner or loved ones. Set aside designated "tech-free" moments to fully engage in each other's presence.

Conclusion

As we conclude our exploration of love and intimacy in the digital world in "Love in the Digital Age," we have uncovered the ways in which technology has redefined the landscape of emotional and physical closeness. We've celebrated the benefits of virtual intimacy, from accessibility to creativity, while acknowledging the challenges it presents, such as screen mediation and privacy concerns.

In the chapters that follow, we will continue our journey through the evolving landscape of love in the digital age. We will delve into the complexities of trust and transparency in digital relationships, explore strategies for addressing conflicts that arise in digital interactions, and discuss the importance of balancing our digital and offline lives. As we navigate this digital realm of love, let us remember that technology can enhance but never replace the authenticity, empathy, and genuine connection that define true intimacy. Whether we're sharing a virtual moment or embracing in person, the heart of love remains unwavering in its quest for closeness and connection.

7

Love in the Digital Age

Trust and Transparency Online

Introduction

As we continue our journey through "Love in the Digital Age," we arrive at a pivotal juncture where trust and transparency take center stage. In the realm of digital relationships, where screens mediate our interactions, trust becomes the bedrock upon which lasting connections are built. In this chapter, we will navigate the intricacies of trust and transparency in digital relationships, addressing the insecurities and challenges that can arise while offering strategies for building trust and fostering open communication.

Navigating Trust Issues and Insecurities in Digital Relationships

Trust is a fundamental aspect of any relationship, but in the digital realm, it takes on unique dimensions and complexities. Let's explore the common trust issues and insecurities that can surface in digital relationships.

1.1. Trust in the Digital Age

Trust in the digital age encompasses several aspects:

- Identity Verification: With the potential for online deception, individuals may question the authenticity of the identities of those they meet online.
  - Privacy Concerns: Concerns about personal information and privacy breaches can lead to feelings of vulnerability and mistrust.
  - Digital Infidelity: The ease of connecting with others online can raise concerns about emotional or physical infidelity in digital relationships.
  - Communication Consistency: Trust can be affected by the consistency and reliability of digital communication, including response times and frequency.

1.2. Insecurities in Digital Love

Insecurities can be amplified in the digital realm. Individuals may grapple with feelings of inadequacy or jealousy based on the online interactions of their partners. These insecurities can strain relationships and hinder trust.

Building Trust and Fostering Open Communication

Building trust in digital relationships requires intention, effort, and a commitment to transparency and authenticity. Here are strategies for fostering trust and open communication online.

2.1. Authenticity is Key

Authenticity is the foundation of trust. Be genuine and transparent in your digital interactions. Share your thoughts, feelings, and intentions openly with your partner.

2.2. Respect Boundaries

Respect your partner's boundaries and privacy preferences. Discuss and establish boundaries together, and ensure you both feel comfortable with the level of sharing in your digital relationship.

2.3. Consistent Communication

Consistency in communication is vital for building trust. Make an effort to respond promptly to messages, and communicate openly about your availability and expectations regarding communication frequency.

2.4. Address Insecurities

If insecurities arise, address them with empathy and understanding. Encourage open discussions about feelings of jealousy or inadequacy and work together to find solutions that foster trust.

2.5. Honesty About Digital Experiences

Be honest about your digital experiences. If you've connected with someone else online, share this information with your partner. Honesty, even about challenging topics, is essential for trust.

2.6. Empathetic Listening

Practice empathetic listening when your partner expresses concerns or insecurities. Validate their feelings and reassure them of your commitment to the relationship.

Fostering trust and maintaining open communication are ongoing processes in digital relationships. As you navigate the complexities of trust and transparency online, remember that trust is built over time through consistent actions and authentic connections.

Conclusion

As we conclude our exploration of trust and transparency in digital relationships in "Love in the Digital Age," we have unearthed the profound importance of trust in sustaining lasting connections. We've acknowledged the insecurities and challenges that can arise in the digital realm, such as concerns about identity, privacy, and digital infidelity.

But we've also highlighted strategies for building trust and fostering open communication online, emphasizing the central role of authenticity, respect for boundaries, and consistent communication. In the chapters that follow, we will delve into the challenges of long-distance digital love, explore strategies for resolving conflicts that arise in digital interactions, and discuss the importance of balancing our digital and offline lives. As we navigate this digital realm of love, let us carry forward the wisdom that trust is the cornerstone upon which enduring connections are built, and that transparency, empathy, and commitment are the keys to nurturing trust in the age of screens and algorithms.

8

Love in the Digital Age

Challenges of Long-Distance Digital Love

Introduction

In the unfolding narrative of "Love in the Digital Age," we arrive at a chapter that explores one of the most poignant aspects of modern romance: long-distance relationships (LDRs) strengthened by technology. Long gone are the days when geographical separation was an insurmountable barrier to love. Today, digital tools and communication platforms have revolutionized how couples maintain connection across vast distances. In this chapter, we'll delve into the challenges that accompany long-distance digital love and discover strategies for nurturing connection and overcoming the hurdles that distance can bring.

Managing Long-Distance Relationships with the Help of Technology

Long-distance relationships have become increasingly prevalent in our interconnected world. These relationships may emerge when couples live in different cities, countries, or even continents. Technology plays a vital role in bridging the physical gaps and maintaining emotional closeness.

1.1. The Role of Communication Apps

Communication is the lifeblood of any LDR. Messaging apps, video calls, and social media platforms allow couples to stay in touch throughout the day, share experiences, and maintain a sense of presence in each other's lives.

1.2. Virtual Dates and Shared Experiences

Digital tools enable couples to engage in virtual dates and shared experiences despite being physically apart. From watching movies together online to cooking the same recipe over a video call, these activities create a sense of togetherness.

1.3. Creative Expressions of Love

Technology allows for creative expressions of love. Sending surprise virtual gifts, creating digital scrapbooks of shared memories, or even collaborating on playlists that reflect your emotions can deepen the emotional connection.

1.4. Synchronization of Schedules

Managing time zones and coordinating schedules is a common challenge in LDRs. Online tools can help synchronize calendars and plan meaningful moments when both partners are available.

Overcoming Challenges and Nurturing Connection from Afar

While technology offers valuable tools for maintaining long-distance relationships, it also brings forth a unique set of challenges that require understanding and resilience. Let's explore both the challenges and strategies for nurturing connection in LDRs.

2.1. Challenges

- Communication Misunderstandings: The absence of physical cues in digital communication can lead to misunderstandings or misinterpretations of tone.
- Loneliness and Isolation: Geographical separation can lead to feelings of loneliness and isolation, especially during special occasions or holidays.
- Trust and Jealousy: Trust issues can arise due to insecurities, jealousy, or doubts about the faithfulness of a partner who is physically distant.
- Conflict Resolution: Addressing conflicts and resolving disagreements from afar can be challenging, as non-verbal cues are limited.
- Balancing Autonomy: Maintaining individual autonomy while fostering a sense of togetherness can be a delicate balance in LDRs.

2.2. Strategies

- Effective Communication: Clear and open communication is paramount. Encourage honest and regular conversations about feelings, expectations, and challenges.
- Quality over Quantity: Focus on the quality of your interactions rather than the frequency. Make the most of the time you have together, both virtually and in person.
- Shared Goals: Establish shared goals and a vision for the future of your relationship. This sense of purpose can provide motivation and clarity.
- Visit When Possible: Whenever feasible, plan visits to spend physical time together. These visits are essential for maintaining a sense of closeness.
- Trust-Building: Actively build trust by being reliable, transparent, and empathetic. Address insecurities and concerns with patience and understanding.
- Conflict Resolution: Develop effective conflict resolution skills, such as active listening and seeking compromise. Be willing to address issues promptly and constructively.

Conclusion

As we conclude our exploration of the challenges of long-distance digital love in "Love in the Digital Age," we recognize that these relationships, once considered daunting, have been transformed by technology. The hurdles of geographical separation can be overcome with effective communication, shared experiences, and a commitment to trust and empathy.

In the chapters that follow, we will continue our journey through the evolving landscape of love in the digital era. We will explore strategies for addressing conflicts that arise in digital interactions, discuss the importance of balancing our digital and offline lives, and delve into the crucial role of cybersecurity in modern romance. As we navigate this digital realm of love, let us carry forward the wisdom that distance, while challenging, can also deepen our appreciation for the connection we share, and that love, fueled by genuine communication and trust, can flourish across screens, miles, and time zones.

9

Love in the Digital Age

Digital Conflict Resolution

Introduction

In the ever-evolving landscape of "Love in the Digital Age," we arrive at a pivotal chapter that addresses a universal aspect of relationships—conflict. Conflicts are an inherent part of human interactions, and they take on unique dimensions in the digital era. In this chapter, we will explore the intricacies of addressing conflicts that arise in digital interactions and relationships. We will uncover strategies for effective resolution and compromise, emphasizing the importance of empathy, communication, and understanding in navigating the digital conflict landscape.

Strategies for Addressing Conflicts in the Digital Age

Conflict resolution in the digital age requires a nuanced approach that considers the unique challenges presented by online communication. Let's explore strategies for addressing conflicts effectively in digital relationships.

1.1. Active Listening

Active listening is a cornerstone of conflict resolution. In digital interactions, where non-verbal cues are limited, it becomes even more critical. Make an effort to understand your partner's perspective by asking clarifying questions and validating their feelings.

1.2. Choose the Right Medium

Consider the medium of communication when addressing conflicts. Some issues may be better suited for a voice or video call, where tone and nuance can be conveyed more effectively, while others can be discussed via text or messaging.

1.3. Timing Matters

Be mindful of the timing of your discussions. Avoid addressing conflicts when emotions are running high or when either party is busy or distracted. Choose a time when you both can fully engage in the conversation.

1.4. Be Clear and Specific

Clearly articulate the issue at hand and be specific about your concerns. Avoid vague or accusatory language, and focus on describing your feelings and needs.

1.5. Avoid Escalation

In digital conflicts, the absence of face-to-face interaction can lead to misinterpretations. Avoid escalating conflicts by refraining from sarcasm, insults, or inflammatory remarks. Instead, aim to keep the conversation constructive.

1.6. Use "I" Statements

Utilize "I" statements to express your feelings and needs without assigning blame. For example, say, "I felt hurt when I saw that message," rather than, "You hurt me with that message."

1.7. Seek Compromise

Conflict resolution often involves finding common ground and seeking compromise. Be open to finding solutions that accommodate both parties' needs and desires.

1.8. Know When to Take a Break

Sometimes, it's essential to take a break from a conflict to cool off and gain perspective. Discuss with your partner when it might be beneficial to pause the conversation and return to it later.

1.9. Apologize and Forgive

Apologies and forgiveness are powerful tools in conflict resolution. Be willing to apologize when necessary, and practice forgiveness to move forward positively.

1.10. Reflect and Learn

After a conflict is resolved, take time to reflect on what transpired and what can be learned from the experience. Use conflicts as opportunities for personal and relationship growth.

The Digital Conflict Landscape

Conflicts in digital relationships can arise from various sources, including miscommunications, misunderstandings, or differences in expectations. It's essential to recognize the types of conflicts that commonly occur in the digital age.

2.1. Misinterpretation of Messages

Text-based communication can lead to misunderstandings, as tone and context may not be clear. Messages can be misinterpreted, leading to unnecessary conflicts.

2.2. Privacy and Trust Issues

Conflicts related to privacy and trust are prevalent in digital relationships. Concerns about online interactions with others, social media behavior, and privacy breaches can lead to disagreements.

2.3. Technology-Related Conflicts

Conflicts can emerge from differences in technology usage and preferences. For example, disagreements may arise over how frequently to use messaging apps or social media platforms.

2.4. Balancing Offline and Online Life

Finding the right balance between digital interactions and offline life can be a source of conflict. One partner may feel neglected if the other spends too much time online.

Conclusion

As we conclude our exploration of digital conflict resolution in "Love in the Digital Age," we recognize that conflicts are a natural part of relationships, whether they exist in physical or digital spaces. The digital age presents unique challenges, such as the potential for miscommunication and misunderstandings in text-based interactions.

However, by employing strategies for effective conflict resolution—active listening, clear communication, seeking compromise, and practicing empathy—couples can navigate the digital conflict landscape with grace and understanding. Conflict, when approached constructively, can strengthen relationships, deepen understanding, and pave the way for lasting connections in the digital era.

In the chapters that follow, we will continue our journey through the complexities of love in the digital age. We will discuss the importance of balancing digital interactions with offline life, explore the vital role of cybersecurity in modern romance, and reflect on practical ways to nurture meaningful and enduring relationships in a world where screens and algorithms increasingly shape our experiences of love. As we navigate this digital realm of love, let us remember that conflict, when handled with care and respect, can be a catalyst for growth and deeper connection, both online and offline.

10

Love in the Digital Age

Balancing Real and Virtual Worlds

Introduction

In our exploration of "Love in the Digital Age," we've uncovered the profound impact of technology on modern relationships. As we reach this pivotal chapter, we come to a critical juncture where the delicate balance between digital interactions and offline life takes center stage. In a world where screens and algorithms increasingly shape our experiences of love, maintaining a healthy equilibrium between the real and virtual worlds becomes a paramount challenge. In this chapter, we will delve into the complexities of finding this balance and explore strategies for staying present in relationships amidst the myriad distractions of the digital age.

Maintaining a Healthy Balance

The digital age has ushered in unprecedented connectivity, allowing us to interact with loved ones and potential partners across distances. However, this connectivity can sometimes come at the cost of our presence in the offline world. Let's explore why it's crucial to strike a balance between the digital and real worlds.

1.1. The Power of Digital Connections

Digital connections offer convenience, accessibility, and the ability to stay connected with people near and far. They provide opportunities for virtual dating, maintaining long-distance relationships, and accessing support networks.

1.2. The Risks of Digital Overload

While digital connections are valuable, excessive screen time and constant connectivity can lead to issues such as digital addiction, decreased face-to-face interaction, and a sense of disconnection from the physical world.

1.3. The Importance of Real-World Presence

Balancing digital interactions with real-world presence is essential for maintaining meaningful relationships. Being fully present during in-person moments fosters deeper connections and enhances the quality of time spent together.

Strategies for Staying Present in Relationships

Maintaining a balance between the digital and real worlds requires mindfulness and intentional efforts. Here are strategies for staying present in your relationships amidst digital distractions.

2.1. Set Digital Boundaries

Establish boundaries for your digital interactions. Designate specific times for checking messages, emails, or social media, and commit to being fully present during face-to-face interactions.

2.2. Practice Digital Detox

Periodically disconnect from your devices to recharge and refocus on the physical world. A digital detox can help you appreciate the value of offline moments.

2.3. Cultivate Mindfulness

Practice mindfulness in your daily life. Be present in the moment, whether you're on a date, spending time with family, or engaging in a hobby. Mindfulness enhances the quality of your interactions.

2.4. Prioritize Face-to-Face Time

Prioritize in-person interactions with loved ones. Schedule regular date nights, family gatherings, or outings with friends to strengthen real-world connections.

2.5. Unplug During Important Moments

When sharing significant life events or intimate moments with loved ones, make a conscious effort to put away your devices and fully engage with the experience.

2.6. Digital-Free Spaces

Create digital-free spaces in your home or designated areas where screens are not allowed. These spaces can serve as sanctuaries for genuine interaction.

2.7. Communicate Your Intentions

Communicate your intentions with your loved ones. Let them know when you're unplugging or focusing on digital-free interactions to avoid misunderstandings.

2.8. Practice Gratitude

Express gratitude for the moments you share with loved ones. Recognize the value of these offline connections in a world saturated with digital distractions.

Conclusion

As we conclude our exploration of balancing real and virtual worlds in "Love in the Digital Age," we acknowledge the complexities of maintaining a healthy equilibrium in a digital-centric society. While digital connections offer numerous advantages, they must coexist harmoniously with the richness of offline experiences.

In the chapters that follow, we will continue our journey through the evolving landscape of love in the digital era. We will explore the crucial role of cybersecurity in modern romance, reflect on the enduring nature of love in the digital age, and offer practical advice for nurturing meaningful, enduring relationships. As we navigate this digital realm of love, let us remember that technology, while a powerful tool, should never overshadow the profound beauty of genuine, present, and authentic connections in the real world. It is in the harmonious balance between the digital and the tangible that we find the true essence of love in the modern age.

11

Love in the Digital Age

Cybersecurity in Love

Introduction

In our journey through "Love in the Digital Age," we've explored the transformative impact of technology on modern relationships. As we embark on this chapter, we confront an essential aspect of digital romance: cybersecurity. The digital age brings new opportunities for love, but it also introduces vulnerabilities and risks that require careful navigation. In this chapter, we will delve into the critical importance of protecting personal information and privacy in the digital age, along with strategies for managing the challenges of online security in relationships.

Protecting Personal Information and Privacy

The digital age has ushered in an era of unprecedented interconnectedness, but it has also heightened concerns about privacy and security. Let's explore the significance of safeguarding personal information and privacy in the realm of modern romance.

1.1. The Digital Footprint

Every digital interaction leaves a trace, creating a digital footprint that can be accessed by others if not adequately protected. Personal information, such as contact details, photos, and relationship status, is valuable and should be safeguarded.

1.2. Privacy Concerns

Privacy concerns in digital relationships include the risk of data breaches, online stalking, identity theft, and the potential misuse of personal information. These concerns can lead to stress and anxiety in online interactions.

1.3. The Importance of Consent

Consent plays a vital role in digital relationships. It is essential to obtain consent before sharing personal information, images, or intimate details. Respecting boundaries is key to building trust.

1.4. Protecting Against Scams

Online romance scams are a significant concern in the digital age. Individuals should be cautious when engaging with new online acquaintances and remain vigilant against potential scams.

Strategies for Navigating Online Security in Relationships

Online security is paramount in digital relationships. Employing strategies to protect personal information and privacy ensures a safe and trustworthy online environment. Let's explore strategies for managing the challenges of cybersecurity in love.

2.1. Secure Passwords

Use strong, unique passwords for online accounts, and consider using a password manager to keep track of them. Change passwords regularly and enable two-factor authentication whenever possible.

2.2. Protect Personal Information

Exercise caution when sharing personal information online. Avoid disclosing sensitive details, such as your home address or financial information, to individuals you've just met online.

2.3. Verify Identities

Before sharing personal information or engaging in intimate conversations with someone online, take steps to verify their identity. Be cautious of individuals who refuse to provide clear information about themselves.

2.4. Use Secure Communication Channels

Use secure messaging apps and platforms that offer end-to-end encryption to protect the privacy of your conversations. Avoid sharing sensitive information over unsecured channels.

2.5. Educate Yourself

Stay informed about common online scams and cybersecurity threats. Awareness is your best defense against potential risks.

2.6. Report Suspicious Activity

If you encounter suspicious behavior or believe you are the victim of a scam, report it to the relevant authorities or platform administrators. Prompt action can prevent further harm.

2.7. Trust Your Instincts

Trust your instincts. If something doesn't feel right in an online relationship, take a step back and reassess the situation. It's better to be cautious than to risk your security.

2.8. Communicate Openly

Maintain open communication with your partner about online security concerns. Discuss strategies for protecting your privacy and information, and ensure you both feel safe in your digital interactions.

Conclusion

As we conclude our exploration of cybersecurity in love in "Love in the Digital Age," we recognize the vital importance of protecting personal information and privacy in the digital realm. The digital age offers opportunities for meaningful connections, but it also presents vulnerabilities that require vigilance and caution.

In the chapters that follow, we will continue our journey through the evolving landscape of love in the digital era. We will reflect on the enduring nature of love and offer practical advice for nurturing meaningful, enduring relationships. As we navigate this digital realm of love, let us remember that love, when built on a foundation of trust and respect, can flourish securely in the digital age, allowing us to embrace the transformative power of technology while safeguarding our most valuable asset—our personal privacy and security.

12

Love in the Digital Age

Cultivating Lasting Love in the Digital Era

Introduction

As we near the conclusion of our journey through "Love in the Digital Age," we arrive at a chapter that serves as a beacon of reflection and guidance. Love in the digital era, though intricately influenced by technology, retains its core essence—a profound, enduring connection between two individuals. In this chapter, we will contemplate the evolving nature of love in the digital age and offer practical advice for nurturing meaningful, enduring relationships amidst the ever-changing landscape of screens, algorithms, and virtual connections.

Reflections on the Evolving Nature of Love

Love has existed as a powerful force throughout human history, transcending cultural shifts and technological advancements. In the digital age, love takes on new dimensions and complexities.

1.1. Technology as a Catalyst

Technology serves as a catalyst for love, allowing individuals to connect, communicate, and explore relationships in ways unimaginable in the past. It expands the horizons of romantic possibilities and enhances the depth of emotional connection.

1.2. The Digital Paradox

The digital age presents both opportunities and challenges for love. While technology enables connection across vast distances, it can also lead to feelings of isolation and superficial interactions if not managed mindfully.

1.3. The Importance of Authenticity

Amidst the digital noise, authenticity remains the cornerstone of lasting love. Authentic connections forged through genuine communication, empathy, and vulnerability stand the test of time.

1.4. Adaptation and Growth

Love in the digital age requires adaptation and growth. Couples must navigate changing dynamics, from long-distance relationships to digital conflict resolution, while staying committed to the core values of trust, respect, and understanding.

Practical Advice for Nurturing Meaningful Relationships

Nurturing meaningful relationships in the digital era involves a blend of timeless principles and modern insights. Let's explore practical advice for cultivating lasting love in the digital age.

2.1. Prioritize Communication

Effective communication is the bedrock of any relationship. Make an effort to communicate openly, honestly, and empathetically with your partner. Create spaces for deep conversations, both online and offline.

2.2. Balance Digital and Offline Life

Maintain a balance between your digital interactions and your offline life. Dedicate quality time to in-person moments, as these are the foundation of enduring connections.

2.3. Embrace Vulnerability

Vulnerability is a powerful force in love. Share your thoughts, fears, and aspirations with your partner. Vulnerability fosters intimacy and deepens your connection.

2.4. Cultivate Trust

Trust is essential in any relationship. Build trust through consistency, transparency, and a commitment to respect each other's boundaries.

2.5. Be Mindful of Digital Boundaries

Establish and respect digital boundaries in your relationship. Discuss what is acceptable and what should remain private in your online interactions.

2.6. Prioritize Quality Over Quantity

Focus on the quality of your interactions rather than the quantity. Meaningful moments and genuine connections are more valuable than superficial exchanges.

2.7. Support Each Other's Growth

Encourage and support each other's personal growth and aspirations. Healthy relationships allow individuals to flourish as they pursue their dreams.

2.8. Celebrate Milestones

Celebrate milestones and create meaningful memories together. Whether it's anniversaries, special occasions, or personal achievements, commemorate moments that matter.

2.9. Practice Gratitude

Express gratitude for the love and connection you share. Regularly remind your partner of your appreciation and affection.

2.10. Adapt and Learn

Be adaptable and willing to learn as your relationship evolves. Embrace change as an opportunity for growth and deeper connection.

Conclusion

As we conclude our exploration of cultivating lasting love in the digital era in "Love in the Digital Age," we recognize that love, while influenced by technology, remains a timeless and profound force. In a world where screens and algorithms increasingly shape our experiences of love, it is the enduring values of communication, trust, authenticity, and vulnerability that continue to define the depth and longevity of our connections.

In this final chapter, we have offered practical advice for navigating the complexities of love in the digital age, emphasizing the importance of meaningful communication, digital-life balance, and the nurturing of trust and vulnerability. As we bid farewell to this journey, let us carry forward the wisdom that love, whether expressed through a virtual message or a tender embrace, remains a beacon of hope and connection in a rapidly changing world. May we cherish the enduring nature of love and nurture it with care, compassion, and the enduring power of human connection.

Summary: Love in the Digital Age

In the dynamic landscape of human relationships, the digital age has wrought transformative changes, offering both opportunities and challenges. "Love in the Digital Age" is a comprehensive exploration of how technology has reshaped modern love, emphasizing the importance of understanding, adapting, and nurturing meaningful connections in an era defined by screens, algorithms, and virtual encounters.

Chapter 1: The Transformative Impact of Technology on Modern Love
This chapter provides historical context and evolution of digital communication in relationships, highlighting how technology has shaped the way we connect and interact in the modern world.

Chapter 2: Digital Dating Dynamics
Exploring the landscape of online dating platforms, this chapter offers strategies for crafting authentic profiles and navigating digital dating etiquette.

Chapter 3: Virtual Courtship and Connection
The art of building meaningful connections in virtual spaces is examined here, along with insights into navigating the challenges and benefits of virtual relationships.

Chapter 4: Navigating Online Communication
Effective communication in the era of texts, emojis, and GIFs is discussed, emphasizing the role of tone and context in digital conversations.

Chapter 5: Social Media's Role in Modern Romance

This chapter examines the impact of social media on dating and relationships, offering strategies for maintaining healthy boundaries and authenticity online.

Chapter 6: Love and Intimacy in the Digital World
The concept of intimacy is redefined through technology and virtual experiences, with guidance on cultivating emotional closeness in an era of digital connections.

Chapter 7: Trust and Transparency Online
Navigating trust issues and insecurities in digital relationships is the focus, with strategies for building trust and fostering open communication.

Chapter 8: Challenges of Long-Distance Digital Love
Managing long-distance relationships with the help of technology is explored, along with guidance on overcoming challenges and nurturing connection from afar.

Chapter 9: Digital Conflict Resolution
Strategies for addressing conflicts that arise in digital interactions are detailed, including the utilization of technology for effective resolution and compromise.

Chapter 10: Balancing Real and Virtual Worlds
This chapter emphasizes the importance of maintaining a healthy balance between digital interactions and offline life, offering strategies for staying present in relationships amidst digital distractions.

Chapter 11: Cybersecurity in Love
Protecting personal information and privacy in the digital age is discussed, along with insights into navigating the challenges of online security in relationships.

Chapter 12: Cultivating Lasting Love in the Digital Era

The concluding chapter reflects on the evolving nature of love in the digital age and provides practical advice for nurturing meaningful, enduring relationships.

"Love in the Digital Age" serves as a comprehensive guide for anyone navigating the complexities of modern romance. It recognizes that while technology has reshaped how we connect, the enduring values of communication, trust, authenticity, and vulnerability remain the bedrock of lasting love in a rapidly changing world.

www.ingramcontent.com/pod-product-compliance
Lightning Source LLC
LaVergne TN
LVHW012128070526
838202LV00056B/5920